FLUSH

Celebrating Bathrooms Past & Present

Photographs & Text by

Steve Gottlieb

To Anne, with whom I happily share a bathroom.

Published by Privy Publishing

98 Bohemia Ave., Ste 3 • Chesapeake City, MD 21815 • www.privypublishing.com

ISBN: 978-0-615-90364-4

Book Design: Steve Gottlieb • Printed in China

Bulk purchases and personalized covers of FLUSH, fine art prints and stock usage of book images: **steve@gottliebphoto.com.**

Steve Gottlieb's photography workshops: **www.horizonworkshops.com**

Photos: p.1: Baltimore, MD (Evergreen Museum & Library);
p.2: Jerome, AZ (Mining Museum); p.7: Boulder City, AZ (Little City Grille)

Other Books by Steve Gottlieb

Abandoned America

American Icons

Washington: Portrait of a City

Cecil County: A Personal Portrait

↙ Restrooms ↘

WOMEN · MEN

Restrooms

LADIES
Welcome

Women/girls

Men's Room

EMPLOYEES MUST
WASH HANDS BEFORE
RETURNING TO WORK

FLUSH is one photographer's exploration of the bathroom or, if you prefer, restroom...lavatory...toilet...john...powder room... mens room...ladies room...womens room...boys room... girls room...latrine...urinal...outhouse...can...throne...washroom...facilities...comfort station...loo...crapper...public convenience...head...privy...potty...water closet (W.C.)...commode.

The vast number of synonyms—euphemisms really—that we've devised for the bathroom surely reflects our culture's high degree of discomfort bordering on taboo. (1960s Hollywood Production Code: movie violence, okay; toilet flushing, no way.) On average, we spend one entire year of our lives on the toilet—and thousands more hours in the bathroom showering, bathing, shaving, tweezing, brushing, flossing, combing and otherwise making ourselves more presentable to the world. Yet most of us prefer not to talk about the bathroom... or see, smell, touch, hear or even think about what takes place inside.

To create FLUSH, I threw my own discomfort downwind and poked my nose—and camera—into all manner of bathrooms. Grungy to gilded, minute to massive, outhouses to airplanes. What I've chosen to include between these covers are bathrooms (and their contents) that struck me as unusual, impressive or historic. They caught my eye and made me think... smile...wonder...gasp. The result is a personal, and admittedly quirky, collection of images, accompanied by my idiosyncratic musings. Bear in mind that I approached bathrooms as a visual person with almost no knowledge of their inner workings. My aesthetic judgments were not influenced by any significant understanding of plumbing, hygiene, civil engineering, hydrology, chemistry, environmental science, toilet manufacture, archeology, cultural anthropology or bathroom history.

The bathroom, as everyone knows, is generally the blandest room in the house...the office...the hotel...the restaurant...the museum. Bathrooms are usually designed for functional, not aesthetic, reasons. *But that doesn't have to be so!* Bathrooms can be gorgeous, exciting, fun, expressive, enchanting, distinctive. However, in creating FLUSH, I discovered that it takes some effort—and roadwork—to find them.

And how did I find them? Many of the best location ideas came after I mentioned my project during my workshops and photo talks; people invariably came up to me afterward with specific suggestions. Online research pointed the way to other locations. Finally, serendipity lent a hand—I simply stumbled upon places in the course of my meandering. As for gaining access to locations, that was usually easy. People with unusual bathrooms were, with rare exceptions, delighted to have them photographed.

A word about the genesis of FLUSH. Taking pictures of bathrooms had never been a particular focus of mine. During my travels, if I saw interesting bathrooms or bathroom-

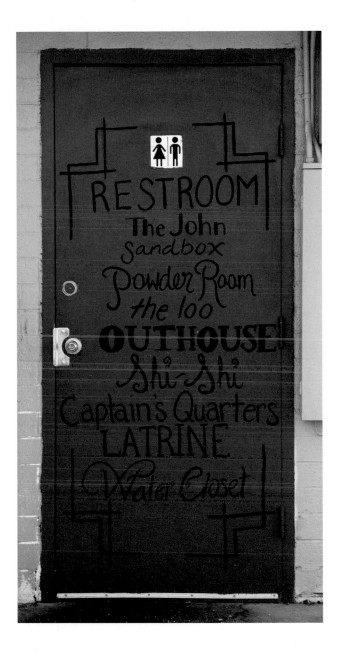

related subjects, I photographed them just as I photographed anything that caught my eye. A few years ago, I decorated my photography workshop's bathroom walls with prints of bathroom subjects; I also included some bathroom images in various presentations. The enthusiastic reaction to these pictures revealed a significant—though rarely expressed—interest in the subject. That gave me the idea that people might enjoy a book of images. For the next couple of years, bathrooms became one of my photographic objectives. I feel like I've been on an extended, adventurous treasure hunt... with a highly unusual objective.

Creating this book has been immensely satisfying. FLUSH, along with my four other books, are the highlights of my photographic career. Not only do I love exploring subjects in-depth with my camera, but books give me a rationale for scratching my wanderlust itch...and meeting local denizens in the process. "Any really unusual bathrooms around here?" is, I learned, a sure-fire conversation-starter.

As with all book projects, there comes a time to flush the last flush and close the lid. Now it's time to share my "bathroom odyssey" with you.

Steve Gottlieb

OUT OF THE PAST

Eons before the first flush was flushed...millennia before the first outhouse was built...when nature called, nature itself provided the venue for relief. Even today, all of us, at one time or another, have left our personal imprint upon the land just as Neanderthal and Cro-Magnon man once did.

At some point—who knows when—outhouses were built in order to permit comfortable sitting, provide privacy, minimize contact with weather and animals, and avoid depositing waste helter-skelter near the living area. [Location: Bodie, California]

Outhouse Essentials

■ Outhouses were located downwind from the buildings they served—here it was a South Dakota church—and downhill from the well.

■ Hole size was precise—too large and the user might slip down, too small and the user might miss the target.

■ After the pit was filled, the outhouse was pushed over a new hole; the dirt from the new hole was spread over the old hole...and boards were often laid on top to prevent accidents.

■ Toilet paper was rarely used. Depending on location, season, availability and social customs, cleaning options included: rags, wood shavings, leaves, grass, hay, sand, moss, water, maize, ferns, fruit skins, snow and, most commonly in the U.S., corncobs or pages from a Sears Catalog.

■ Between 1933 and 1945, workers from the Works Project Administration (a Depression-era public works program) built or refurbished 2 million outhouses...for $5.00 or less.

■ In rural areas, outhouses were commonly used until the 1950s. Today, they are no longer a common sight; the few that still stand are rarely used...at least not for their original purpose.

■ The outhouse, observed one expert, is "arguably the most environmentally-correct device ever developed for disposing of human waste. It requires no water, no electrical energy, no plastic or copper plumbing, no sewers to overflow or rupture and it pollutes no river."

■ The pit often served as a receptacle for discarded household items, not just human waste. Researchers excavate them for clues about how people lived. Sound like fun? You can join the National Privy Diggers Association.

■ Like bathrooms, outhouses spawned a very long list of euphemistic synonyms, including: backhouse, crapping kennel, dooley, garden loo, honey bucket, little house, reading room, shooting gallery, thinking room, throne, waterloo and the you-know-where.

■ Today, outhouses have a substantial cult following in the United States. Once, they were routinely burned or torn down; now they're collected, and even sold...and they are the focus of books, calendars, wallpaper, birdhouses and more. A yearning for simpler times, perhaps?

If required to sit thigh-to-naked-thigh with someone else while going to the bathroom, most people would be aghast. But in the 1870s, if you were waiting for a train at Harbeson Station, Delaware, and nature called, you might well find yourself doing just that.

Two-hole outhouses were not uncommon back then...and plenty were built with three or more holes. This particular outhouse [at right], now re-located to historic Lewes, Delaware, is rare because it has two "two-holers" back-to-back—four people could sit under the same tiny roof with just a thin, common wall between two pairs of two holes.

Here's a scenario for a Western spoof like Blazing Saddles: Two gunslingers about to face each other in a showdown—both so nervous they had to relieve themselves first—sharing a two-holer. Humor aside, sitting on the toilet with clothes around our ankles is a highly vulnerable posture.

[Left: Seligman, AZ]

Many historic homes proclaim, "George Washington Slept Here," but only one authoritatively proclaims: "George Washington Sat Here." (Actually, this one was rebuilt.) The Father of Our Country designed his "necessary," as he called it, with three holes; he probably sat side-by-side with Martha, the kids...and perhaps some of the hundreds of guests they entertained every year. George's privies were partially made of brick and designed to be permanent; unlike most outhouses, there was no need to ever move it...he had slaves to keep it cleaned out.

In 1856, famed Senator and diplomat Henry Clay, also a slaveholder, elevated the permanent privy to the size of a small house at "Ashland," his Lexington, KY estate. It had three rooms... two for two two-holers and one for laundry. This privy continued in use into the 1920s.

How far should an outhouse be placed from the main building? It's a balancing act.

Close offers convenience, as with this home in Lancaster County, PA...

...while far reduces unpleasant odors, as with this adobe church in Abiquiu, New Mexico.

When it's cold, wet or dark, who wants to tromp out to the outhouse? Hence the chamber pot (or slop jar), which sat beside or under the bed or was hidden—in plain sight—within a (sometimes airtight) compartment, in this case the second step of a small bedside ladder. Pots were also commonly hidden inside chairs and other furniture.

Chamber pots date back to at least the 6th century BC, and were used until indoor plumbing arrived—in the late 19th century in the city and in the mid-20th century in rural areas. Rural folks generally dumped the contents into the garden (good fertilizer) or into the outhouse pit, while city dwellers usually hurled the waste into the fetid streets. (Walking under a second story window in the morning when pots were being emptied was risky; people would shout, "gardez l'eau"—watch out for the water—but possibly too late for a pedestrian to react.)

Pots were usually painted with lovely designs; in Victorian times, they were even treated as art objects. Royalty owned, and traveled with, pots of silver or gold that reflected their social status. Today, chamber pots are considered collectibles.

[Pot: Fanshawe Pioneer Village, London, Ontario.
Steps: Arlington House, Robert E. Lee's home.]

If there's a source of water extremely close by, you don't need an outhouse or chamber pot. Man learned very early to use water to flush away waste, so if you ran water under your building you could locate the bathroom inside. You just needed to make sure that waste water flowed downstream and cooking was done upstream—otherwise, you might contract typhoid, cholera or dysentery, among other diseases. Early Romans understood these sanitation basics, but when they left Britain in 450 AD, their sanitation knowledge apparently went with them. For the next thousand years, Britain plunged into the (sanitary) Dark Ages. Clearly, technological and medical progress doesn't always flow in a straight line...especially when cultural taboos are involved.

The Bunratty Castle in southwest Ireland, circa 1425, was the site of this early interior toilet. The primitive "plumbing" for this spartan, but spacious, facility was a moat approximately three stories below. Because moats did not always have a regular infusion of fresh water, the odors, it was said, could be over-whelming...but, looking on the positive side, that increased the moat's effectiveness as a deterrent to would-be invaders.

400+ years after Bunratty Castle was built, this (reconstructed) facility inside Fort Delaware, located on an island in the lower Delaware River, shows no evidence of advances in plumbing. The same basic system was used—drop your waste down into the moat below...whose water was "refreshed" by tidal currents. This fort served as a Civil War POW camp. Confederate POWs were housed in cramped barracks outside the fort and never had access to this "high end" toilet, which was available only to Union soldiers stationed inside.

Two notable signs of technological progress since Bunratty: First, instead of a stone seat, this one is made of wood, which is warmer for the buns in winter. (Some early stone seats were designed to capture warmth from nearby fires.) Second, the sitter could enjoy something to read, like the popular Harper's Weekly. At Bunratty, at least in its early years, it was unlikely there was anything to read since the printing press had not yet been invented.

Toilet Time Line

■ Evidence of toilets made of bricks and wood, with chutes leading to street drains or a cesspit, dates approximately to 3000 BC.

■ Flush toilets with flowing water connected to a sophisticated sewage system appeared in the Indus Valley [Pakistan/Afghanistan] around 2600 BC and in Crete in 1700 BC.

■ Flush toilets were used throughout the Roman Empire from 100 to 500 AD. There was no privacy—just stone seats next to one another without any partitions. (An early Roman privy that has survived to this day has a line-up of eight holes.)

■ The next milestone appears to have been a thousand years later, in 1592, when the godson of Queen Elizabeth I designed the first fully functioning, self-contained waste disposal fixture. It had a seat, a bowl to receive the waste and a cistern [water receptacle] to flush the waste away. The Queen refused to even try it and the innovation was quickly forgotten.

■ 200 years later, Alexander Cumming invented the first toilet (called the Valve Closet back then).

■ In the mid-1800s, the Thames River was an open sewer; it was called the time of the "Great Stink." This led Queen Victoria to support construction of a modern sewer system and spurred several inventors to develop the "modern" toilet. Ceramic became the material of choice, since lead, copper, and zinc were difficult to clean. The modern bathroom industry was born.

■ In the 1860s, permanent plumbing fixtures appeared in buildings with water supply and drainage, replacing portable basins, buckets, and chamber pots. For most people of that era, a full-body wash only occurred a few times a year.

■ The modern bathroom, equipped with a sink, tub, and flush toilet was an early 20th-century development. (These items were called "fixtures" because they were in fixed positions.) That was when people first began to appreciate the relationship between bodily filth and germs...and germs and disease. These relationships were known earlier, but the science wasn't established with absolute certainty, so people were slow to change their toilet habits. White fixtures were used because they made it easier to see dirt; ceramic made it easy to clean. Initially, rooms designed to promote personal hygiene were almost unheard of, except for the very wealthy.

■ One expert calculated that bath fixture installation costs, plus water usage fees, plus processing by waste treatment plants (paid for with our tax dollars), results in a cost of about forty to fifty cents per flush. Some folks spend more. Dirk Kempthorne, George W. Bush's Secretary of the Interior, contributed to toilet history in 2007 by spending $222,000 taxpayer dollars renovating his government office bathroom, which he used less than two years.

[Right: Allegheny Mountains home.]

Deep in the woods, just a mile from my studio, is a long-abandoned sawmill which doubled as the owner's eclectic junk yard. Featuring items like an old toilet seat and rusty cast iron bathtub, it's my photo workshop students' favorite place. One student struck a "Rodin's Thinker" pose. At right, that's me taking a ghostly "leaf bath."

Ceramic bowls are virtually indestructible unless broken or ground up. Unlike cast iron tubs, they don't oxidize. Used ones have no value. This bowl might well remain in the same spot and in the same condition for eons, available for future photographers to use in their own creative ways.

The most common way I found locations for FLUSH was simply to tell people that I was working on the book. Many people—people who would otherwise have no reason to discuss bathrooms with me—responded with an astonishing number of specific and excellent ideas. My friend Bud Thomas, who is in the process of renovating and redeveloping an enormous abandoned factory in northern Delaware, invited me for a visit when I told him about FLUSH. His factory has many photogenic bathrooms, including this unusual two-person "trough urinal." Another one of "Bud's bathrooms" is the cover image.

In busy washrooms, urinals are installed for efficiency: com-
pared with a toilet, a urinal takes less space and consumes less
water per flush. And doors and locks aren't needed—at most,
privacy barriers might be installed, as seen here.

The last man who peed here did so in 1955. That was the
year that Packard Motors, once a major name in the automo-
bile industry, closed its jaw-droppingly huge Detroit plant that
boasted 47 buildings totaling 3.5 million square feet spread
across 35 acres. The plant was the most modern of its time when
it opened in 1903. At its peak, it employed 40,000 workers; wan-
dering through the plant, I could feel their ghostly presence.

One recent observer of this shuttered plant noted: "Scav-
engers often broke in to cut power and phone lines for scrap
copper. Vandals seem to be in a race with Mother Nature to see
who could destroy the building the fastest." That disheartening
commentary would apply to many of the abandoned places in
this book...fortunately for this photographer, no one ever steals
a toilet or urinal. A silent irony: the small "Wet Paint" sign has un-
doubtedly hung in the same spot for more than half a century.

"Workers always dropped their boots and gloves in the locker room at the end of the day," explained my guide, the former plant manager of the paper mill. "One night after they went home, they were told the plant was permanently closed. The place has been locked up tight ever since...so everything stayed where it was." (I moved the boots and gloves a few feet.)

I have always had passionate feelings about abandoned things, from faucets to factories and well beyond. That led me to create an entire book on the subject, *Abandoned America.* My workshop students all seem to share my passion; they love taking pictures at the abandoned sawmill

and similar places.

What is the underlying source of these feelings? I can't speak for others, but for me, abandoned things act like a magic carpet that transports me to different historical times and places. I often sense the phantom presence of people long gone. It's like going back in time, but without the problems one would actually have leaving the present. Here's another reason for these feelings: Things whose time has come and gone stir a sense of my own mortality. "Preserving" these abandoned things in a "permanent" photographic book, provides me, the photographer, a sense—or illusion—of grasping a glimmer of immortality.

Needing storage space, businessman Barry Stup purchased an enormous decommissioned military warehouse at the Army's Letterkenny Depot in Pennsylvania. The basement included a typical military-style toilet line-up.

Military folks always use the word latrine. They should never use the word "privy," which comes from the Latin "privatus," meaning private. That is not something the military believes in, at least in this context. Historically, bathroom privacy was not always the overwhelming preference it is in today's society. In some European countries in the 1800s, it was considered appropriate to receive visitors while sitting on the pot. Times change.

Speaking of word derivation, the word "toilet" comes from the French word "toile," which refers to the act of washing, dressing, and preparing oneself. As the years passed, the word evolved into denoting the room or facility in which one arranges their toilet... and then further evolved to being recognized as the room where one—to grab another euphemism—"went to the bathroom."

Why do toilets always have hinged seats? You don't want to sit on something that somebody may have dribbled on.

A few short blocks from downtown Philadelphia stands the imposing Eastern State Penitentiary, which had the distinction of being the largest public building in America when it was built in the 1830s. Back then, every prisoner lived in isolation, a Bible his only companion. Isolation, it was believed, led to penitence (hence penitentiary), though lunacy was the more likely outcome. Below: Cellblock 15—"Death Row." (The thin metal grate replaced the original prison door.)

Since its closure in the 1970s, Eastern State remained largely untouched. Now open to tourists, the decayed remnants are compelling, while the posted information can be depressing. Example: The United States is the undisputed leader among all the world's nations in imprisonment per capita.

The epitome of a minimalist bathroom—at least one with plumbing and not in a prison—is seen inside Fire Station No. 1 in Roanoke, VA. Constructed in 1907 and operated continuously until 2007, the building now serves as a museum, infused with atmosphere. Three adjacent sinks are tucked into one corner of the room with three stalls positioned in the facing corner. The bathroom opens up into an expansive room that was home to a few wooden lockers and the traditional fireman's pole used to slide down to the engines below. A circular yellow bar prevents anyone from accidentally falling through the pole hole.

[Next page: An abandoned house in the town where I live is a favorite venue for expressive, albeit redundant, local wordsmiths.]

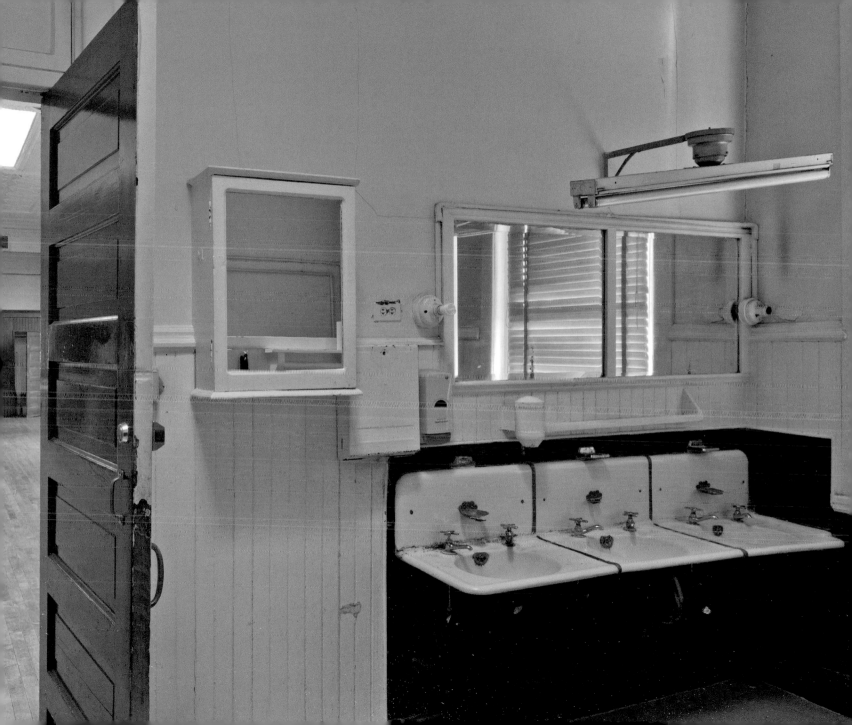

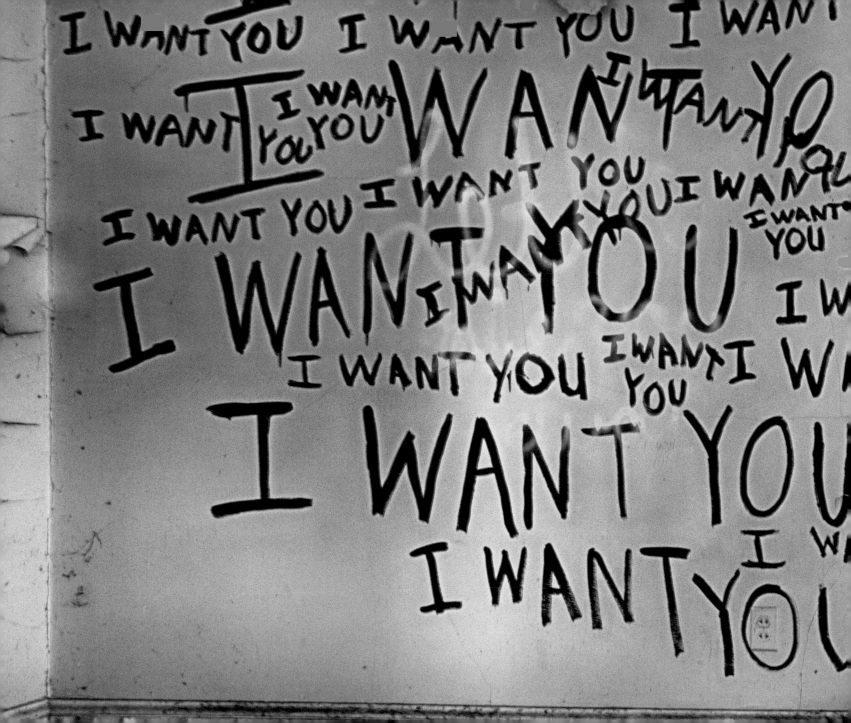

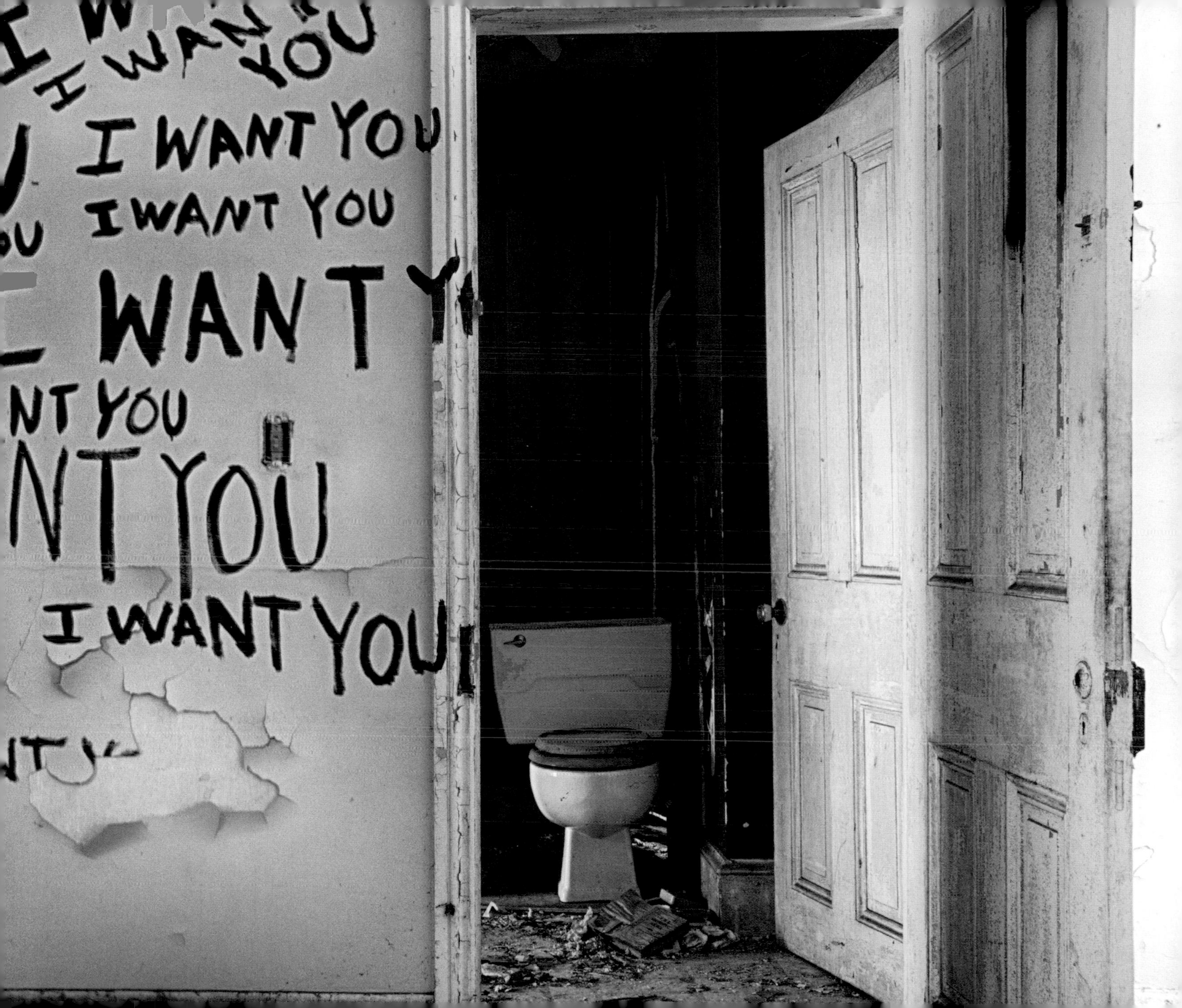
YOU
I WANT YOU
I WANT YOU
WANT
NT YOU
NT YOU
I WANT YOU

[Prior page: In the 1880s, the home of Baltimore's philanthropic T. Harrison Garrett family featured a marble mosaic and gilt bathroom with interior plumbing that provided hot and cold running water, a sitz bath, and a large fireplace to boot. The home is now the Evergreen Museum & Library, owned and administered by The Johns Hopkins University.]

The DC-3 revolutionized long-distance travel when it was introduced in 1936. Twenty-eight people could travel cross-country in 15 hours, which guaranteed they'd use one of these...all 12 square feet of it. Incredibly, some DC-3s remained in service for the next sixty years...presumably with upgraded bathrooms. [Above: Massey (MD) Air Museum]

From 1867 to 1968, if you slept comfortably on a train, you were probably in a Pullman car, which included such luxuries as beds, carpeting, draperies, upholstered chairs, libraries and card tables. These cars also provided an unparalleled level of customer service, thanks to the historically significant Brotherhood of Sleeping Car Porters union. Some Pullman cars boasted toilets and sinks inside individual compartments (most riders shared common bathrooms); the two shown here served adjacent compartments, but a partition could be opened (as it was here) to create a "two room suite" for a family to share. The toilet seat was retractable so it could be hidden inside the cabinet. How, you might wonder, can a toilet be retracted if it is attached to plumbing pipes? The matching signs over each toilet reveal the answer.   [Elgin County Railway Museum, St. Thomas, Ontario]

Evidence of public bath houses—where people could bathe, shower, swim, defecate or socialize—dates to circa 2,000 BC in the Indus Valley [Afghanistan/Pakistan]; Greece and Rome built them beginning around the sixth century BC. The United States was a bit slow getting on the bath house bandwagon. The first was built in the mid-1800s; they didn't flourish until the late 19th century. Bath houses were considered places that would improve health and sanitary conditions, especially for poor people, who had limited access to places to wash themselves.

This massive Art Deco style bath house was built in 1932—a New Deal construction project. For a variety of reasons, bath houses went out of fashion and were all closed (sometimes outlawed) by the 1980s. Those few bath house buildings that still stand, like this one in Jacob Riis Park, Far Rockaway, Queens, NY, are used for other purposes. This building was damaged by Superstorm Sandy and is temporarily boarded up.

Past meets present: an outhouse exterior serves as the entry to an otherwise typical bathroom in a quiet bar in a remote town in central Montana. I mentioned to the bartender that I was a photographer looking for unusual subjects; telling her my special interest was bathrooms seemed too bizarre to mention in this place. I was stunned when she responded, "Before you leave, make sure you use our facilities." (Every language has its share of euphemisms for "I need a place to defecate." Here's a priceless one from China: "I'm going to a remarkable meeting of philosophers and friends.")

When did separate toilets for men and women first appear? It was 1739, when a Parisian restaurant put up "Men Toilet" and "Women Toilet'" signs.

Another past—present combo. Outhouse on the outside, plumbing on the inside. For sheer visual whimsy, you can't beat this double outhouse that the late Juan Delgadillo placed behind his restaurant on historic Route 66 in Seligman, Arizona.

IN THE PRESENT

Bathroom construction was once a one-person effort requiring only basic skills, to wit: the ability to dig a small pit, hammer some boards together, saw a hole or two in a plank, and determine prevailing wind direction. Today, a modern bathroom requires the expertise of a plumber, an electrician, an architect and/or interior designer, and a building contractor...and legions of people who manufacture the room's contents.

Typical modern bathrooms are designed essentially for function, not aesthetics. Fixtures are bland and the room is usually claustrophobically small and barren—often windowless, too, leading one authority to critically observe:

> "After WWII, the mechanical engineers and builders convinced the authorities that a mechanical fan could replace a window. So now you've got fumes from human waste, toxic cleaners, hairsprays and solvents and drain cleaners, all building up in a tiny little room with a closed door and a twelve buck fan that nobody turns on. It really is just dumb."

In contrast to the many distinctive bathrooms found on these pages, here's an example of typical modern bathroom mediocrity. I include it in the spirit of the senator who (infamously) declared in support of a Supreme Court nominee: "So what if he is mediocre? There are a lot of mediocre judges and people and lawyers. They are entitled to a little representation, aren't they?"

Most people decorate their bathroom walls with art—my preference is photographs of bathrooms in my bathrooms. My friends Fred and Starr took quite a different approach. Their bathrooms aren't a place to hang art; rather, they are actual works of art. Their taste is different from mine, to put it mildly...and yet as I photographed this elaborate, over-the-top whimsical design (by artist Laney Oxman), I found myself smitten. What fun...so much to peruse while you're sitting.

In the course of traveling through all 50 states, I've visited many of America's most impressive homes, including the Biltmore in North Carolina, the Hearst Castle in San Simeon, California, and the Breakers in Newport, Rhode Island. They are breathtaking. But the house that most took my breath away is a relatively modest-sized dwelling found in the woods of Sussex County, New Jersey.

Named "Luna Parc" by its owner, Ricky Boscarino, this house—bathroom and all—displays the most extraordinary imagination combined with equally dazzling artistic, design, and construction talents. Luna Parc is all the more impressive because it is a solo effort, in contrast to most spectacular homes, which are huge team undertakings.

The item next to the toilet is a bidet, a common fixture in Europe, but rare in the U.S. One observer caustically observed: "It's odd that we haven't embraced bidets wholeheartedly....If you got poop on your arm, you'd wash it off, not smear it off. And yet, for the butt, we're content to smear....Its name and foreign derivation are clearly some of the reasons for the bidet's unpopularity in the states." P.S. The distinctive chrome shower head in the upper left corner reappears on a later page.

When bathrooms first moved from outhouse to inhouse, they were usually hidden in a utility room. In the 1920s, a number of companies began to promote the idea of a more prominent "decorated bathroom." Consumers fervently (if modestly) embraced the idea of elevating the bathroom beyond its chief purpose—waste removal and sanitation—by giving it some of the decorative attention provided to other rooms in the house.

Today's bathrooms have evolved, in many instances, into highly elaborate showpieces, boasting everything from marble bathtubs to silver faucets (that's the mineral, not the color), to saunas and Jacuzzis®, to TV's and fireplaces...even breathtaking views.

Bathtubs are frequently the centerpiece of the bathroom, but Lloyd Alter, a thoughtful observer of all things bathroom, is no bathtub fan: "It is probably fair to say that the only substantive reason for taking a tub bath (other than pure personal idiosyncrasy) is to 'relax', and yet it is precisely this that the vast majority of tubs have not permitted the user to do, particularly in the U.S....They are too short, they are not comfortable, and there are insufficient grab bars that make them dangerous." (A 1993 study estimated 200,000 bathtub injuries a year.) Furthermore, bathtubs take a long time to fill, consume an immense amount of water and occupy a large footprint.

[Following page: A star attraction at General Sutter Inn in Littitz, PA, is Pearl, a mannequin enjoying an extended bath in the mens room. The owners have kept this room in a funky, unchanged state for decades, except for Pearl's wig or other headgear which is regularly snatched by customers and must be replaced.]

Baltimore's Tremont Hotel, built in 1866, has maintained much of its original elegant flavor, notwithstanding numerous renovations. Its public bathrooms transport one back to a genteel and opulent era. The majestic, classical "Ladies Lounge"—the toilets are in the same room—is fit for royalty.

The sublimely atmospheric Jefferson Hotel, in Richmond, VA, was built in the 1890s and has since been rebuilt. Its renovated bathrooms fit comfortably with the hotel's historic ambience. Patrons of hotels built *before* the 1890s didn't need signs pointing to the bathrooms—they could follow the scent of sewer gas escaping from their early toilets.

One of Las Vegas's many mega-hotels, The Venetian, boasts an interior canal with actual working gondolas. You can gaze down upon the canal from Zeffirino, a restaurant with an ornate, elegant bathroom, whose oversized mirror makes the room even more imposing. Only in Vegas!

"America's Best Restroom" contest, sponsored by the Cintas America company, was a source for some of the locations in FLUSH. Zefferino was one of those deservedly recognized in the contest.

Public restrooms—in Zefferino or wherever—offer a welcome relief to most people, who use them without hesitation. Many people however, suffer from a fear of public restrooms—so many, in fact, that the fear has a name: Lutropublicaphobia. A related phobia is Paruresis—the sufferer is unable to urinate in the (real or imaginary) presence of others. The analogous condition affecting bowel movement is Parcopresis. Such phobias might draw giggles from some, but it's no laughing matter to those afflicted.

In your many visits to restaurant bathrooms, how many hallways/entry areas leading to the bathroom have made a significant impression? If you went to Megu, a restaurant in Manhattan's Tribeca neighborhood, you'd remember. In the space between the mens and womens rooms are two Japanese-style

hanging lamps, surrounded by a series of mirrors that create the illusion of multiplicity. It's the pinnacle of ingenuity. When you stop staring at these "lamps to infinity," and go about your "official" business, Megu's bathrooms continue to create an unforgettable impression.

An extraordinary degree of creativity pulses everywhere in New York City, right down to many of its bathrooms. I could have created a version of FLUSH without ever leaving city limits. Tracy Reese, a Greenwich Village boutique, features a bathroom whose illumination generates a soft glow. Surprisingly, the intensely busy patterns produce a soothing effect.

Smith & MIlls, in New York's Tribeca district, is a bar that's tiny in size but distinctive in character. Its small bathroom features a 100 year-old elevator door that slides open to enter; a pull-down basin from a Pullman railroad car to wash hands; and antique metal work decorating the walls. It's the most eclectic and clever use of materials of any bathroom I've seen.

C. Wonder is one of those hip boutiques that makes window-shopping—and shopping—in NYC's SOHO district such a fun and distinctive experience. The store made the best use of a narrow bathroom footprint by arranging black and white tile in a hypnotic layout. But what's with colored art on the walls? Why not B&W photos?

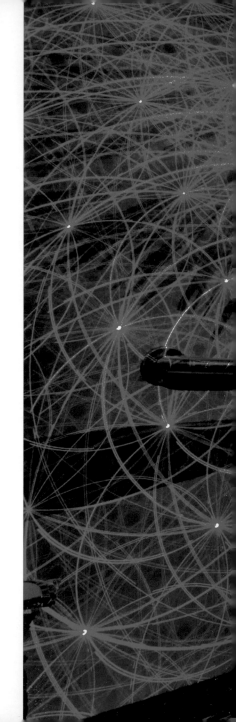

If you're a kid—or a kid at heart—and aren't afraid of the dark, here's a bathroom that turns sitting on the potty into a sci-fi experience. A green laser light dazzlingly dances over the walls and floor. Turn the regular lights on and the walls are covered with lively, colorful illustrations. This playful bathroom is located inside Learning Express in Durham, NC., one branch of a national toy store chain.

Southeastern Pennsylvania's world-famous Longwood
Gardens is home to a world-class restroom "complex"
that, by itself, is worth the price of admission. Lush
plants are brilliantly integrated into a long, curved cor-
ridor, punctuated by a series of individual restrooms. The
restroom interiors (following page), in dramatic contrast
to the organic hallway, make the visitor feel like he/she
has entered a space capsule...or perhaps a time machine.

The bathroom is the only room, at least until the advent
of the cellphone, that guaranteed the opportunity for
quiet contemplation. These sanctuaries at Longwood are a
place where the contemplative mind should soar.

Airplane bathroom design compresses every hygienic essential into the tiniest space, with everything—except two stray rolls of TP—securely anchored in case of turbulence. This is a miracle of human engineering.

When the loo is at least a mile in elevation and the seat-belt sign is turned off, many claim that they've used this cramped space—and first class is no larger—to engage in amorous activities. This is a miracle of human chemistry.

It's been said that inspired architecture has the capacity to generate positive human energy. I believe that can even apply to bathrooms. The two-way entrance/exit of the Wayne County (Detroit) Airport—highlighted by the locally manufactured Peweabic tile—is an example. Few people would be conscious of it, but I think the distinctive undulating shape and beautiful tiles combine to draw one in and lift the spirits.

Space is at a premium on most boats, so "heads" are usually tiny and cramped, as below. But if you happen to own a 76-foot luxury yacht, you've got enough room for a "his and hers"...with roomy shower in between.

Why do boaters always call the bathroom "the head?" In "olden days," boats didn't have bathrooms; a section of the bow was covered with a grate, which was open to the sea below. That's where sailors relieved themselves, their waste falling directly into the water. Other reasons the head was located in the bow: the front of the ship has more (waste-cleaning) water splashing on it...and the (odor-clearing) wind typically blows from stern to bow.

When a sailor needed to relieve himself, he would announce, "I need to go to the head of the ship."

Nowadays, thankfully, most boats of reasonable size have bathrooms, and regulations prescribe how waste must be handled in open water and while docked.

The microflush toilets in boats (and RVs, too), which use air pressure and less water per flush, represent an important technological step forward and should be applied more broadly, suggests one observer.

[Following Page: Library of Congress, Washington, D.C.]

FLUSH celebrates bathrooms, so we won't be exploring their seedier side, as exemplified by many NYC subway station restrooms. (Web surfing yields things like: "Never, ever attempt to utilize the bathrooms in the Astoria Ditmars Blvd N/W or the 57th Street N/R/Q/W stop.") But the vibrant exterior of a Times Square station womens room was too stunning to pass up. I walked by twice during posted hours of operation, but

both times it was closed. A survey found that fully 50% of NYC subway restrooms are closed. Given what might be inside, perhaps it's just as well. At a World Toilet Summit—yes, there is such an event—the American Restroom Association—yes, there is such an association—reported "a general lack of available restrooms for users of public mass transit in the United States due to security concerns and budget constraints."

Pay Toilets: A Capsule History

■ The earliest known pay toilets were erected in Ancient Rome in 74 AD.

■ In European towns in the mid-1600s, wheeled privy carts were available for a fee.

■ The first North American business to install pay toilets was a cafe opened by Walt Disney in 1936.

■ The pay toilet fee—usually a dime or quarter—was not designed to make a profit, but to help defray the costs of cleaning and supplies.

■ Pay toilets were often trashed by patrons and out of paper, and many coin boxes were broken into, all of which rendered them unusable. (Time magazine once declared the pay toilet one of the 50 worst inventions of all time.)

■ Women's groups argued that pay toilets were sexually discriminatory because urinals were free while women were forced to pay to urinate.

■ Homeless people filed a class-action lawsuit in New York to end pay toilets because they couldn't afford them.

■ Because of the many problems and complaints, by the end of the 1970s pay toilets became virtually obsolete in the United States, which added to the sometimes challenging task of finding a public restroom. Pay toilets still flourish in many corners of the world; in the U.S., bathrooms in chain stores and restaurants have made things much better.

■ In January 2008, New York City unveiled its first pay toilet in years—a self-cleaning one—in bustling Madison Square Park (at right). (More are scheduled to be built.) Twenty-five cents buys you fifteen minutes of privacy; then the door automatically opens. I couldn't believe there was no line to get in.

Bathrooms in national and state parks have dramatically increased in number and quality over the years.

The mens and womens room were the only sign of civilization on this sandy beach at the Salton Sea, the largest interior body of water in California. On the pleasantly warm, sunny day I was there, there wasn't a sunbather, swimmer or restroom user in sight. This spot, just three hours from LA and San Diego, has deteriorated from a popular resort destination to something akin to a post-apocalyptic environment...and a fabulous place to take pictures.

The many bathrooms in California's Joshua Tree National Park's camping areas are thoughtfully integrated with the jumbo rock formations.

Tierra Amarilla is a decaying town in northern New Mexico which, incongruously, is home to an exquisitely restored courthouse, a modern town hall/sheriff's office, and the exceptional "Three Ravens" coffee house. Owner Paul Namkung built himself an environmentally low-impact composting outhouse. He was willing to pose on one condition: he didn't have to sit.

The environmentally-conscious Chesapeake Bay Foundation, in Annapolis, MD, installed composting toilets in their offices. These toilets require hardly any water, they reduce the load on sewage treatment plants and the waste is used as fertilizer. (Sign above toilet: "Don't put anything down the chute that you didn't eat first except toilet paper.") I don't know the exact cost-benefit analysis of these "Green Latrines," but it seems we should use more of them wherever practical.

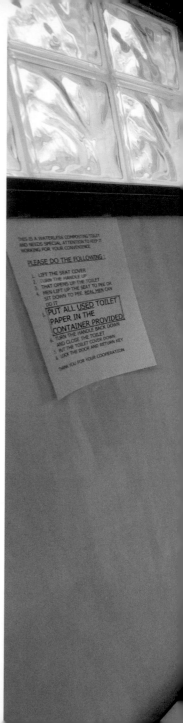

The portable toilet, referred to as a Port-a-Potty or similar name, is one of the greatest low-tech inventions since the wheel. A typical port-a-potty holds enough waste for ten people during the course of a 40-hour work week. They are simple in design and maintenance—they must be drained, cleaned, disinfected, and deodorized on a regular basis. Having no moving parts, they can't malfunction. And they are easy to transport. It's curious that they weren't invented until the 1960s. In one generation, they've gone from nonexistent to omnipresent.

Port-a-Potties make life significantly more comfortable for everyone—like these farm workers in California's Imperial Valley.

One form of creative thinking is finding a productive use for something in an altogether new context. Excellent example: using the external shell of a port-a-potty as a restroom entryway. This installation at Jungle Jim's International Market in Fairfield, OH, is a humorous conversation starter for its patrons. Another creative touch: placing a third port-a-potty between the mens and womens rooms as a "studio" for taking fun portraits—perfect for today's snapshot-driven culture.

The award for "Most Unusual Urinal in the Most Unlikely Place" goes to....Stateline Service Center, an otherwise traditional gas station and food mart near an entrance to Mojave (Desert) National Preserve.

The modest sign on the wall instructs users:

WATERFALL URINAL
ENJOY!!!

And I did!

In my lifetime, I've witnessed the advent of the jet plane, microwave oven, color TV, cell phone, fast food, organ transplants, man on the moon, nuclear energy, personal computer, internet, email, drones, in-vitro fertilization, interstate highways, GPS, digital photography, credit cards, ATMs, DNA mapping, bioengineering, social networking, automatic transmission, 21-speed bicycles, copiers, and diet soda in flip-top cans. Yet over these past decades, the toilet—and the bathroom generally—looks and operates very much like those of a century ago...with the exception of greater color choice. As renowned comedian and actor Jerry Seinfeld might say, "What's up with that?"

ACCESSORIES, PERIPHERALS & BEYOND

The bathroom is not where most people let loose their individuality, creativity and budget. Consequently, most bathroom faucets, knobs and such, like most bathrooms, are pretty mundane affairs—functional and predictable, not worth a second look. There are, however, bathroom accessories that are exquisite and distinctive, like sculpture or jewelry...and sometimes priced accordingly.

When we shower, which shampoo should we choose? Hmmm...decisions, decisions. Amazon sells 2,330 different kinds of shampoo...and that's just for normal hair; it doesn't include shampoos for abnormal hair, hair conditioners, hair coloring treatments or body washes that can double as shampoo. And what about pain relievers, toothpaste, toothbrushes, mouthwash, soap, hairbrushes and toilet paper. Our bathroom presents us with a veritable torrent of decisions.

In *The Paradox of Choice*, Professor Barry Schwartz observes that, paradoxically, those inclined to always maximize the number of options for *every* decision—as opposed the *truly important* decisions—often create greater pressure on themselves and actually diminish their satisfaction. Did I buy the "best" one? Did I get the "best price?" Should I have waited for the new and improved version? So much needless worry...second guessing... time wasted. And for what? The more inconsequential the decision, Schwartz says, the more likely this is to be true.

MILESTONES IN TOILET PAPER HISTORY

■ The first recorded use of toilet paper was in 6th century China.

■ Toilet paper was first mass-produced in the 14th century during the Ming Dynasty.

■ In the United States, the first mass-produced, packaged toilet paper (or bathroom tissue, if you prefer)—replacing dried corn cobs, rags, leaves, Sears catalogs, etc.—appeared in 1857, a mere 1,200 years after initial product development. It was sold in flat sheets. In 1890, Scott Paper introduced tissue on a roll.

■ Americans spend about six billion dollars each year on toilet paper—per person, that's 23.6 rolls, 20,805 sheets and 50 pounds, which is twice the average consumption of western Europeans and Japanese. (Partial reason: American always use paper, never bidets.)

■ Global toilet paper production consumes 27,000 trees daily.

■ Consumers' choices include: one-ply, two-ply, three-ply, soft (a 1942 innovation), extra soft, super soft, squeezably soft, ultra plush, absorbent, softened with aloe, standard, jumbo and mega sizes, quilted, with and without embossed patterns, and colored (especially in Europe). [Curious fact: 60-70% of those surveyed preferred rolls that pull from the top.]

■ Consumer Reports rates toilet paper on the following criteria: Softness; Strength; Disintegration; Tearing Ease.

■ American authors in the 60s and 70s had a fondness for complaining about Europe's waxy, non-absorbent toilet paper; apart from that, nearly all authors steer clear of writing about *any* bathroom subjects.

■ Toilet paper is a favorite object to inflict minor vandalism. Unfurled rolls of toilet paper are thrown over cars, trees, houses, etc., creating a highly visible, though temporary, mess.

■ From 1964 to 1985, and again in 1999, actor Dick Wilson (as Mr. Whipple) pleaded, "Please Don't Squeeze the Charmin" in more than 500 memorably annoying toilet paper commercials. The actual words "toilet paper" or, God-forbid, words that actually describe its purpose, were never spoken.

■ In 1973, Johnny Carson joked: "There's an acute shortage of toilet paper in the United States." Unaware Carson was joking, Americans started a run on toilet paper that caused a nationwide shortage for three weeks.

YOU DON'T HAVE TO BE A MEMBER OF MENSA TO CHANGE THE TOILET ROLL

Living rooms, bedrooms, dining rooms and kitchens mirror, in some measure, our taste and style. But the room that surely reveals the most about us is the bathroom. The items we gather here, and especially in the medicine cabinet, speak volumes about what ails us, how worried we are, whether we have trouble sleeping, whether we have problems with "regularity" (an exquisite example of bathroom euphemeze), how we choose to smell, how we choose to groom ourselves, and so much more.

Mikey, the cat, knows all, but he ain't tellin'.

Decades ago, graffiti in mens public restrooms was common-place. (I'm told this was true for ladies rooms, too.) Generally, the words and drawings were crudely sexual in content and devoid of originality, humor or artistry. In what is surely a positive, though modest, cultural shift, this form of self-expression and advertising has dramatically diminished over the years. Why? Perhaps toilet authors/artists are engaging in welcome self-restraint; or maybe wall finishes are more difficult to write on; or perhaps bathroom owners are more proactive about eradicating offensive missives.

None of these restraints has operated at the Cat's Eye Pub in Baltimore's Fell's Point, whose proprietor(s) has taken a laissez-faire attitude since the bathroom walls were first used as a writer's canvas more than thirty years ago. Notwithstanding the plethora of considerably repugnant and inane scribblings, the accumulated graffiti has transformed the walls into something akin to a marvelous piece of communal art.

Everyone of us, at one time or another, has had an urgent need to go to the bathroom. Restroom signs spell RELIEF. The variety of these signs has dramatically diminished over the past few decades, replaced by simple, universal symbols— you don't even need to speak the local language. Unfortunately, universality eliminates distinctiveness and creativity.

Right: Dog Track, Canyon City, AZ

For distinctive restroom signs, you can't beat "South of the Border," a gloriously garish tourist attraction in South Carolina. Once aptly voted the "Tackiest Place in the Mid-Atlantic," SOTB has a powerful appeal, especially for kids and color photographers.

These are the first two bathroom-related photos I ever took, some twenty-six years ago. According to one observer, SOTB has survived for over six decades because of the owners' astute ability to adapt to ever-changing consumer tastes. I wonder if these wonderful signs still exist? Maybe they've been replaced—groan!— by universal symbols.

In 1906, inventor William Sloan developed a system using pressurized water directly from the supply line for faster recycle time between flushes. To this day, many flush mechanisms bear his name. Because there is zero recharge time, the next user has no wait time, making flushometer toilets especially useful for public restrooms, like this urinal in the National Building Museum, Washington, D.C. (Ladies, those orange thingies are plastic filters that keep gum and other detrius from gumming up the plumbing.)

Relatively recently, there has been a small, but notable, improvement to the "flushometer:" the infrared-triggered automatic flush (above). As to how the trigger knows when and when not to flush—that is something beyond my low plumbing/engineering IQ.

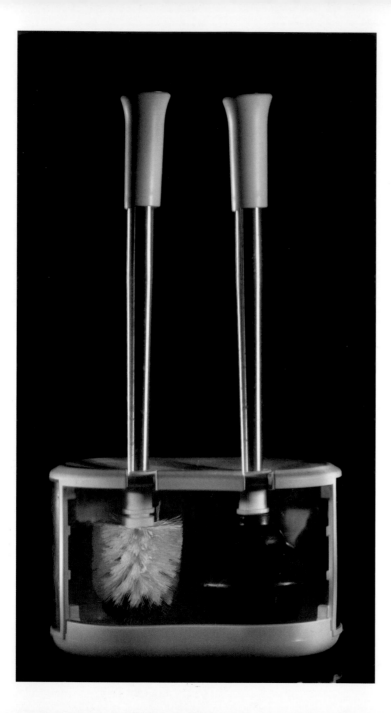

With the help of a wrench and rubber washer, I've success-fully managed to fix a leaky faucet or two, but the only bath-room tools I use with real confidence are the plunger and toilet brush. Whenever there's a significant leak or other problem in the bathroom, I'm helpless. I call my trusty plumber, Tommy, who works his magic with assuredness and enthusiasm.

"Over my 40 years as a plumber," says Tommy, "there've been improvements in bathroom technology, like low-flow toilets and urinals that use a lot less water. But the plumbing basics... they haven't changed much." The major reason is probably a cultural resistance to changing our approach to bathrooms.

After you flush, what happens to your feces, excrement, fecal matter, bowel movement, BM, crap, defecation, excreta, dung, manure, number two, stool, poop, pooh-pooh, turd, caca, doo-doo, droppings, shit? (Comedian George Carlin loved to point out that while these all mean the same thing, you can't say the last one on TV!) Here's the poop about the treatment of poop (and urine, too):

■ The average adult generates more than 400 pounds of this stuff every year, along with 500 quarts of urine. Despite this impressive output, few people give the "post-flush" universe much thought.

■ Poop was once a valuable commodity, used for such things as fertilizer and making saltpeter (gunpowder component). Urine was used for bleaching wool, leather tanning and treating certain medical conditions (urine is sterile when it leaves the body). "Pole men" collected waste from privies in vats, carried on a pole. In some places, it was a sophisticated, competitive business. In Japan, fights erupted over collection rights and prices, and there were incidents of waste theft. Interestingly, the waste of rich people—who had better diets—had greater value as fertilizer.

■ At the turn of the century, awareness that diseases, including cholera, typhoid and dysentery, were related to inadequate waste disposal motivated cities to build sewer systems that transported waste to nearby rivers... and, later, to plants where wastewater is treated to separate and dispose of the waste component and "recondition" the water so we can once again drink it...or reuse it to flush our toilets.

■ Today, there are over 16,000 publicly-owned treatment facilities in the U.S. The way we use water and treat wastewater raises a number of challenges in the view of many experts, such as:

1. We waste high-quality drinking water (as opposed to "grey water") when we use it to flush away our waste. [Using grey water for flushing would, of course, require separate pipes.]

2. We don't use the waste components productively.

3. We use too much valuable water to move waste into the treatment system. Notably, Australian Bruce Thompson developed the Duoset toilet tank in 1980, with two buttons and two flush volumes, which can save the average household 67% of their normal toilet water usage. This tank is rarely used, though there have been some other notable improvements in water usage.

One of the most pressing challenges in the world is neither improving toilet efficiency nor wastewater treatment. It's helping the 2.5 billion people in the world who lack access to basic sanitation...and saving some of the 1.5 million children who die every year as a result. Of the world's 7 billion people, 6 billion have access to mobile phones, while only 4.5 billion have access to working toilets. Of the 2.5 billion who lack proper sanitation, 1.1 billion defecate in the open (which can contaminate water supplies). This is a global public health crisis that doesn't get adequate attention, in part because the subject makes people uncomfortable.

Two bright spots in this bleak landscape: The World Toilet Organization was founded in 2001 with a mission to "improve sanitation conditions for people globally through powerful advocacy, inventive technology, education and building marketplace opportunities locally." The WTO established World Toilet Day, organizes the annual World Toilet Summit and provides relevant training through the World Toilet College.

Another bright spot is the Bill and Melinda Gates Foundation "Reinvent the Toilet" challenge; meeting the challenge would improve sanitation, water quality, land values, human dignity and more. Substantial grant money is being awarded to universities and research institutions to develop a stand-alone toilet designed to meet these rigorous criteria: (a) hygienic, odor-free, safe, easy to install and doesn't require piped-in water, external electricity or linking to a sewer; (b) converts feces and urine into usable resources (electricity, fuel or fertilizer); (c) costs less than 5¢ per use; and (d) requires limited maintenance/cleaning.

With toilet design basically unchanged since the first flush toilet patent was issued in 1775, the time is ripe, says the Foundation, for dramatic innovation. "Many of these innovations will not only revolutionize sanitation in the developing world," Bill Gates predicted, "but also help transform our dependence on traditional flush toilets in wealthy nations."

One of many R&D groups around the world working to meet the Gates Foundation challenge is a team at Research Triangle Institute (Brian Stoner, team leader, center; Dayle Johnson (lab coat); Ethan Klem). The Foundation's grant money—to RTI and many others—represents more than just financial support; it adds a certain gravitas to working in a field that too often generates smirks, giggles, double entendres and punch lines. (I confess to feeling awkward telling my friends that my career has taken a turn toward toilet photography.) If we want more technological progress, we need less bathroom embarrassment.

"I have been photographing our toilet, that glossy enameled receptacle of extraordinary beauty," wrote legendary photographer Edward Weston in 1925. "Here was every sensuous curve of the 'human figure divine' but minus the imperfections."

Weston was surely exaggerating—especially if you're familiar with his nude images—but his core point is significant. He found aesthetic beauty in a mundane object that most everyone takes for granted. That perspective was ground-breaking back then, which is why it now costs upwards of $10,000 to purchase an original print of "Excusado," the title he gave to his toilet image. In the same vein, Marcel Duchamp's "Fountain," an everyday urinal laid on its side and signed by the artist (using a false name), was deemed the 20th century's most influential work of art in a 2004 survey of 500 experts.

These two photos—the one on the left is a newly developed waterless/flushless urinal—owe a debt of gratitude to Weston and Duchamp. In the spirit of "Excusado" and "Fountain" I hope that FLUSH stimulates a greater awareness of, and appreciation for, the humble toilet, its precursors, its bathroom companions, and bathrooms in general.

Good flushing to one and all.

References

More words—many thousands times more—have been written about what we ingest than what we excrete. To those relatively few people who have written about the "flush universe," I am grateful for your research and insights. I list your work below (alphabetical by author). Since this is a photography book that makes no pretense to being a formal analysis, I hope I'll be forgiven for not specifically referencing you in the text and/or footnotes.

Ronald Barlow, *The Vanishing American Outhouse* • Dottie Booth, *Nature Calls: The History, Lore and Charm of Outhouses* • Bob Cary, *The All-American Outhouse* • Penny Coleman, *Toilets, Bathtubs, Sinks and Sewers* • Deuce Flanagan, *Everybody Poops 410 Pounds a Year* • Julie Horan, *The Porcelain God: A Social History of the Toilet* • P. Nicole King, *Sombreros and Motorcycles in a Newer South* • Lupton and Miller, *The Bathroom, the Kitchen and the Aesthetics of Waste* • Londie Garcia Padelsky, *Outhouses: Flushing Out American's Hidden Treasures* • Dave Praeger, *Poop Culture*.

These internet sources were also valuable:
A series of articles by Lloyd Alter, including: www.treehugger.com/bathroom-design/the-history-of-the-bathroom-part-3-putting-plumbing-before-people.html • www.bathroom-association.org/pdf/toiletstory-p1.pdf • www.theplumber.com/#history 5 • www.localhistories.org/toilets.html (Tim Lambert) • www.sometimes-interesting.com/2011/08/15/largest-abandoned-factory-in-the-world-the-packard-factory-detroit/ • www.sulabhtoiletmuseum.org • http://www.amny.com/urbanite-1.812039/flush-with-filth-many-subway-station-bathrooms-dirty-or-locked-up-1.1857262 • www.answers.yahoo.com/question/index?qid=20060824102949AAO3ULG • www.en.wikipedia.org/wiki/Sleeping_car • www.en.wikipedia.org/wiki/Public_bathing • www.en.wikipedia.org/wiki/Flushometer • www.wikipedia.org/wiki/toilet_paper • www.bestrestroom.com (Contest sponsored by Cintas America) • www.todayifoundout.com (Eddie Deezen, 8/23/12) • www.wiki.answers.com/Q/Why_is_a_bathroom_a_head_on_a_boat (Bill Hempel) • www.newsfeed.time.com/2013/03/25/more-people-have-cell-phones-than-toilets-u-n-study-shows/#ixzz2U9HvcLap

Acknowledgements

I want to express my admiration for those interior designers, architects, builders, plumbers and proprietors/developers, etc. who created these wonderful bathrooms and bathroom components.

I want to thank all those who had location suggestions and/or who helped me find, and get access to, these locations. In addition to those previously named, here are some others: Stephanie Adams, Willima Meredith, Bud Thomas, Fred & Starr, Jimmy Crawford & Lisa Bistreich-Wolfe, Joe Ciluffo, James Abbot, Rich Frances, Phyllis Berger, Dawn Bonner, Stephanie Adams, Akiko Kitajima, Akiva Elstein, Cecilia Liotine, Charlotte Howard, Ralph and Clare Hazel, Yitzhak Elhadad.

Finally, I am grateful to those friends and colleagues who offered their advice, support and talents: Rahsaan Jackson, who contributed his formidable Adobe Indesign® and Photoshop® skills; my son Jason, for his creative insights; Tracy Mitchell Griggs and Diane Shapiro, for valuable editorial help; and, finally, my partner Anne Constant, for her unwavering and loving encouragement.

Steve Gottlieb is the photographer/ author of the widely acclaimed books, *Abandoned America, American Icons* and *Washington: Portrait of a City*. Literally thousands of photographs from his books and assignments have been published worldwide. In 2005, Steve founded Horizon Photography Workshops, which *American Photo* magazine selected as one of the "12

Awesome Travel Workshops in the United States." (*www.horizonwork-shops.com*) He is a frequent speaker on photography and creative/ innovative thinking. A graduate of Columbia University's College and Law School, Steve practiced law in private firms and the federal government before turning his photography hobby into a vocation. Father of two sons, Steve divides his time between Chesapeake City, MD and Washington, D.C.